PUBLISHING

READING
ACTIVITIES

Develop enthusiastic readers through the study of character, plot and setting

IDEAL FOR
APP ✓
ASSESSING PUPIL'S PROGRESS

BOOK
2

Years 3–4   Suzi de Gouveia

Title:	Sensational Reading Activities
Author:	Suzi de Gouveia
Editor:	Paula Wagemaker
Book Code:	PB00047
ISBN:	978-1-908735-31-7
Published:	2012
Publisher:	TTS Group Ltd
	Park Lane Business Park Kirkby-in-Ashfield Notts, NG17 9GU Tel: 0800 318 686 Fax: 0800 137 525
Websites:	www.tts-shopping.com
Copyright:	Text: © Suzi de Gouveia, 2008
	Edition and Illustrations: © TTS Group Ltd, 2012

About the author:

Suzi de Gouveia is a full-time classroom teacher with international experience. She has had the pleasure of teaching in a multi-cultural environment and is passionate about English.

Suzi would like to thank Heulwen Roberts for her assistance and support while completing this book. She would also like to thank Diggs for doing the housework.

Contents

Introduction

Sensational Reading Activities contains clear and engaging worksheets that save teachers time and labour. The copiable worksheets can be used with a variety of texts that include stimulating follow-up activities related to guided and independent reading and covering different aspects of literature.

Sensational Reading Activities is suitable for pupils in Years 2 and 3 and is designed to build and develop comprehension through the study of character, plot and setting. The worksheets can be applied to both fiction and non-fiction texts and interpreted in a variety of ways to cater to the needs of your pupils. Other worksheets focus on problem-solving, comparing, vocabulary, presenting, book reports and thinking skills.

Curriculum links

Literacy	
Learning Strand Year 2	**Objectives:** *Most children will learn to:*
7. Understanding and interpreting texts.	• Draw together ideas and information from across a whole text, using simple signposts in the text • Use syntax and context to build their store of vocabulary when reading for meaning
8. Engaging with and responding to texts	• Explain their reactions to texts, commenting on important aspects.
Year 3	*Most children will learn to:*
7. Understanding and interpreting texts.	• Identify and make notes of the main points of section(s) of text • Infer characters' feelings in fiction and consequences in logical explanations • Use syntax, context and word structure to build their store of vocabulary as they read for meaning • Explore how different texts appeal to readers using varied sentence structures and descriptive language.

Source: Adapted from the *Primary Framework for Literacy and Mathematics*, 2006

Plot

Make a sequence chart.

Title: _____

Author: _____

```
┌─────────────┐        ┌─────────────┐
│             │   →    │             │
│             │        │             │
└─────────────┘        └─────────────┘
                              ↓
┌─────────────┐        ┌─────────────┐
│             │   →    │             │
│             │        │             │
└─────────────┘        └─────────────┘
      ↓
┌─────────────┐        ┌─────────────┐
│             │   →    │             │
│             │        │             │
└─────────────┘        └─────────────┘
```

Name: _____

5

Title: _____

Author: _____

Draw a picture and write a sentence about the four most important events in the story.

1.	2.

3.	4.

Name: _____

Plot

Title: _____

Author: _____

Draw your favourite part of the story. Write about your picture.

Name: _____

Plot

Title: _____

Author: _____

Draw a cartoon strip showing the main events of the story.

Have you remembered speech bubbles?

Name: _____

Plot

Title: _____

Author: _____

Write a letter to the publisher suggesting a change to the plot. You must give the publisher reasons for your suggestion.

Name: _____

Setting

Draw a picture about where the story took place.
Remember to show the details. Write about your picture.

_____

_____

_____

_____

_____

_____

_____

Name: _____

Setting

Title: _____

Author: _____

This is where my story took place.

Describe the setting here:

Name: _____

Setting

Title: _____

Author: _____

Where does the story take place?

This is where the story takes place in the beginning...

In the beginning...

This is where the story takes place at the end...

the end!

Name: _____

Setting

Title: _____

Author: _____

1. Where does the story take place? Describe the main setting.

2. Could there really be a place like this? Why?

3. How does the setting influence the story?

4. Which part of the story describes the setting the best?

5. When does the story take place (past, present or future)?

6. Draw the main setting.

Name: _____

Setting

Make a map of your book. Remember to label the important places clearly.

Name: _____

Setting

Title: _____

Author: _____

Draw the main setting of the book in one oval. Draw the neighbourhood where you live in the other oval.

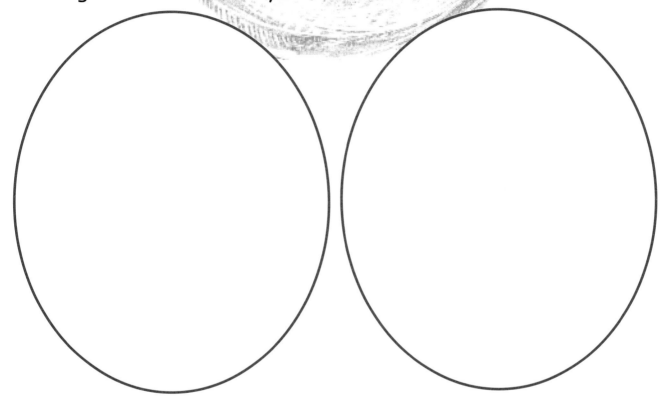

Write about the differences or similarities.

_____

_____

_____

_____

_____

Name: _____

Setting

Read three books and fill in this chart.

	Title	Place	Time of Day	Weather
1.				
2.				
3.				

Name: _____

Setting

Draw the main setting of the story in the picture frame.
Write a sentence about the setting in each box.

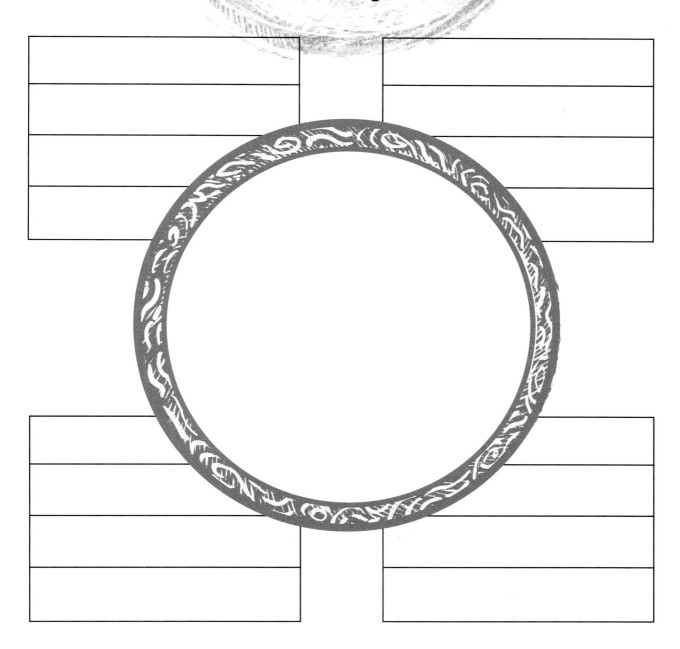

Character

Title: _____

Author: _____

Publisher: _____

Write a letter to one of the characters in the story.
Tell the character what you like about his or her actions

_____

_____

_____

_____

_____

_____

_____

_____

_____

_____

Name: _____

Character

Title: _____

Author: _____

Publisher: _____

Write down the names of all the characters in the story.

_____   _____

_____   _____

_____   _____

_____   _____

Name the main character and write two or three sentences describing this character. Use interesting words to describe the character.

_____

_____

_____

_____

_____

_____

Name: _____

Character

Title: _____

Author: _____

Publisher: _____

Draw one or some of the characters in this book. Label the characters. Write some adjectives to tell more about them.

Name: _____

Character

Title: _____

Author: _____

Publisher: _____

Here is some information about my favourite character in this book.

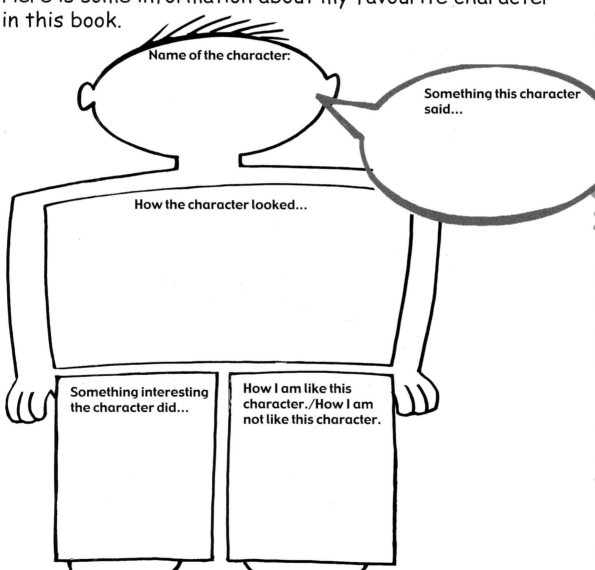

Name of the character:

Something this character said...

How the character looked...

Something interesting the character did...

How I am like this character./How I am not like this character.

Name: _____

Character

Title: _____

Author: _____

Publisher: _____

Personality profile for ....

Name: _____

Character

Title: _____

Author: _____

Publisher: _____

Draw one of the characters. Write about your picture.

_____

_____

_____

_____

_____

_____

Name: _____   23

Character

Title: _____

Author: _____

Publisher: _____

Compare two of the characters in the book.

Character one:	Character two:

Name: _____

Character

Title: _____

Author: _____

Publisher: _____

Draw the main character of the story in the picture frame. Write a sentence about the character in each space.

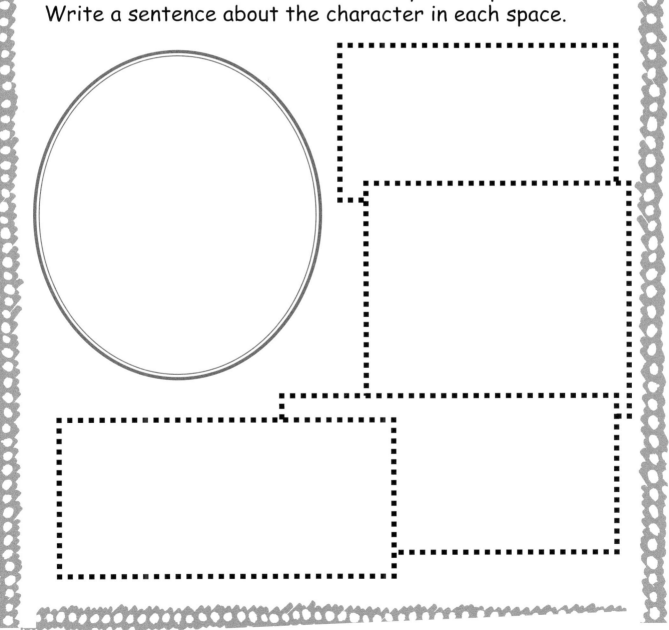

Name: _____

Character

Title: _____

Author: _____

Illustrator: _____

Compare the main character in this story with one of your friends. Write five words to describe each one. Use interesting adjectives to do a good job.

Main character	My friend
1.	1.
2.	2.
3.	3.
4.	4.
5.	5.

Name: _____

Character

Title: _____

Author: _____

Illustrator: _____

Remember to be respectful!

Compare the main character in this story with one of your parents or guardians. Write five words to describe each one.

Main character	Parent / Guardian
1.	1.
2.	2.
3.	3.
4.	4.
5.	5.

Name: _____

Character

Title: _____

Author: _____

Illustrator: _____

Design the main character's bedroom. Label your design and give reasons for your choices.

```
┌ ─ ─ ─ ─ ─ ─ ─ ─ ─ ─ ─ ─ ─ ─ ─ ─ ─ ─ ─ ┐
|                                        |
|                                        |
|                                        |
|                                        |
|                                        |
|                                        |
|                                        |
├ ─ ─ ─ ─ ─ ─ ─ ─ ─ ─ ─ ─ ─ ─ ─ ─ ─ ─ ─ ┤
| Reasons                                |
|                                        |
|                                        |
|                                        |
|                                        |
└ ─ ─ ─ ─ ─ ─ ─ ─ ─ ─ ─ ─ ─ ─ ─ ─ ─ ─ ─ ┘
```

Name: _____

Character

Title: _____

Author: _____

Illustrator: _____

Look in some magazines and find words that tell you about the main character or a secondary character of this story. Stick these words onto this page. Only use words that tell you about the character.

Name: _____

Character

Title: _____

Author: _____

Illustrator: _____

Make up five interview questions for the character. Then write the answer you think the character would give.

Question	Answer
1.	
2.	
3.	
4.	
5.	

Name: _____

Character

Title: _____

Author: _____

Setting

Problem and Solution

Title: _____

Author: _____

Draw pictures to show a problem in the story and the solution to it.

The problem...

The solution...

Name: _____

Problem and Solution

Title: _____

Author: _____

Write about the problem and the solution.

The problem in this story...	The solution to the problem...

Name: _____

Problem and Solution

Title: _____

Author: _____

Can you think of a better or different solution to this problem? Write or draw your idea and give reasons why you think it might be better.

Name: _____

Comparing Stories

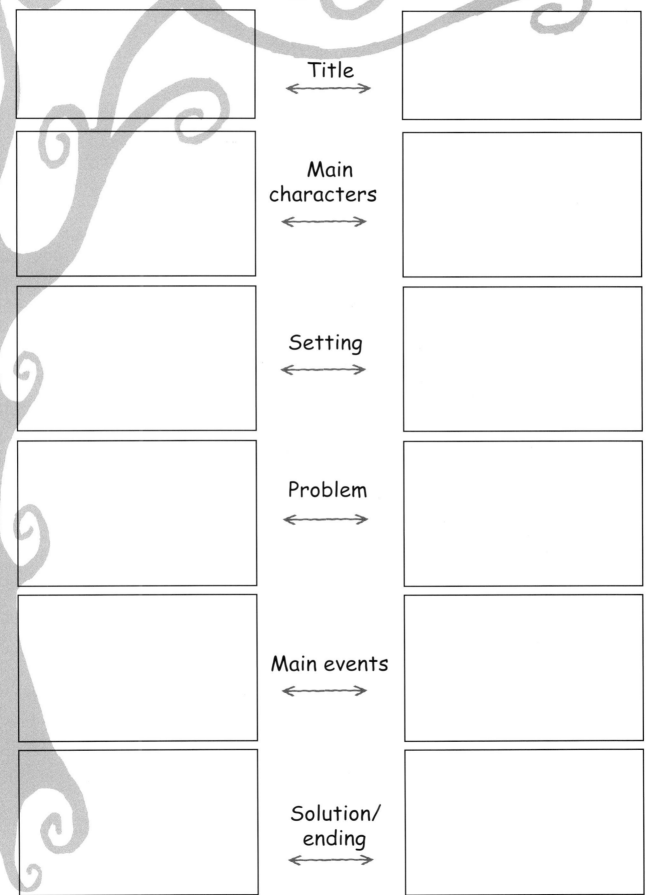

Title ←→

Main characters ←→

Setting ←→

Problem ←→

Main events ←→

Solution/ ending ←→

Name: _____

Non-fiction

Title: _____

Author: _____

Publisher: _____

What did you learn from this book?

_____

_____

Draw and label what you have learned.

Name: _____

Non-fiction

Title: _____

Author: _____

Publisher: _____

Finish this web so as to show what you have learned from this book.

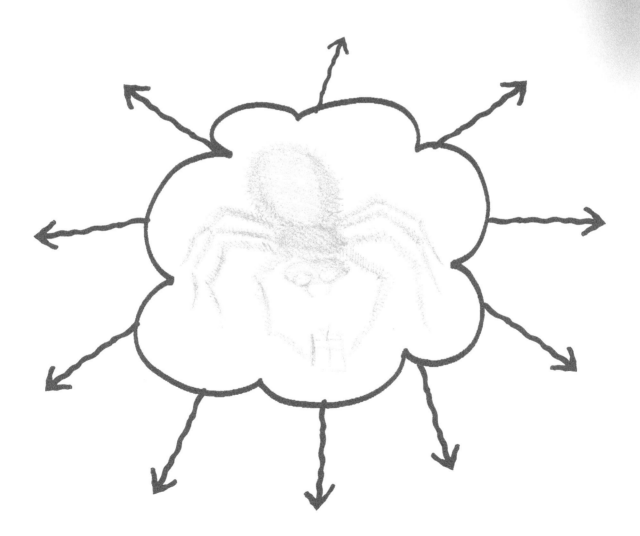

Name: _____

Non-fiction

Title: _____

Author: _____

Publisher: _____

What questions do you have about this subject? Write them down here.

_____

_____

_____

_____

_____

Find an expert or another book to help you answer the questions you have. Write the answers here.

_____

_____

_____

_____

_____

_____

Name: _____

Non-fiction

Title: _____

Author: _____

Publisher: _____

What other books can you find on this subject? Look in the library and make a list. Remember to write down the publisher of the book.

Well done!

Name: _____

Non-fiction

Title: _____

Author: _____

Publisher: _____

I know...

Name: _____

Non-fiction

Title: _____

Author: _____

Publisher: _____

I have learned these facts about...

☆   ☆

☆   ☆

☆   ☆

☆   ☆

Name: _____

Title: _____

Author: _____

Publisher: _____

Habitat
_____
_____
_____

Food
_____
_____
_____

Babies
_____
_____
_____

Name: _____

Non-fiction

Title: _____

Author: _____

Publisher: _____

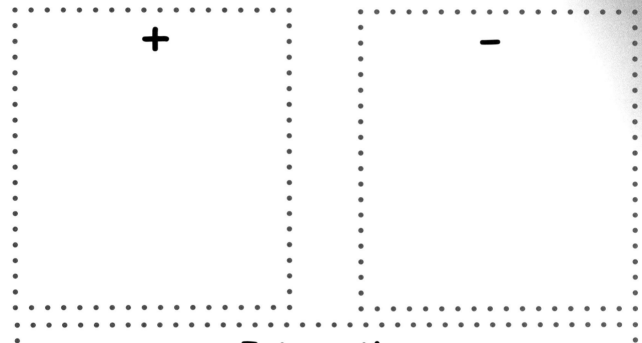

+	−

Interesting

Name: _____

Non-fiction

Title: _____

Author: _____

Publisher: _____

Think of five questions to ask another person in your class about this book. Write the questions here.

1. _____

_____

2. _____

_____

3. _____

_____

4. _____

_____

5. _____

_____

FANTASTIC!

Now ask a friend to find the answers by reading the same book.

Name: _____

Vocabulary

Write a list of words that are about the subject of your book. Put these words into alphabetical order. Write a definition about each word. Make a small dictionary using these words.

List	Alphabetical Order	Definition

Name: _____

Vocabulary

Write down any new or interesting words you read in this story.

Write each word in a sentence that shows the meaning of the word.

_____

_____

_____

_____

_____

_____

Great job!

Name: _____

Vocabulary

Find, write and illustrate some of the compound words in this book. One is done as an example for you...

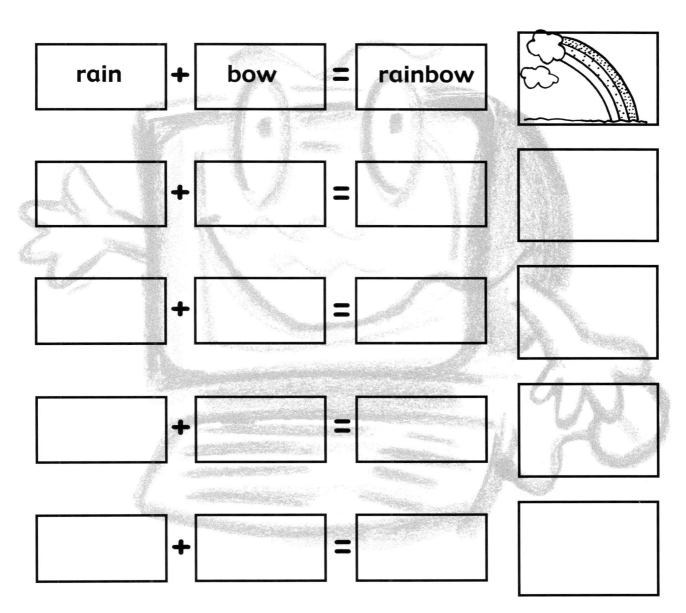

rain	+	bow	=	rainbow

© TTS Group Ltd, 2012

Vocabulary

Write a list of contractions in this book. Show how these contractions are formed.

isn't → **is not**

_____ → _____

_____ → _____

_____ → _____

_____ → _____

_____ → _____

_____ → _____

_____ → _____

Name: _____

Presenting

Design a book cover for this book.

Have you remembered the author and illustrator?

Name: _____

Presenting

Make a wanted poster for a character in this book.

Wanted!

Name: _____

Presenting

Design and make a bookmark for this book.
Give it to someone you think should read this book.

Name: _____

BOOK REPORT

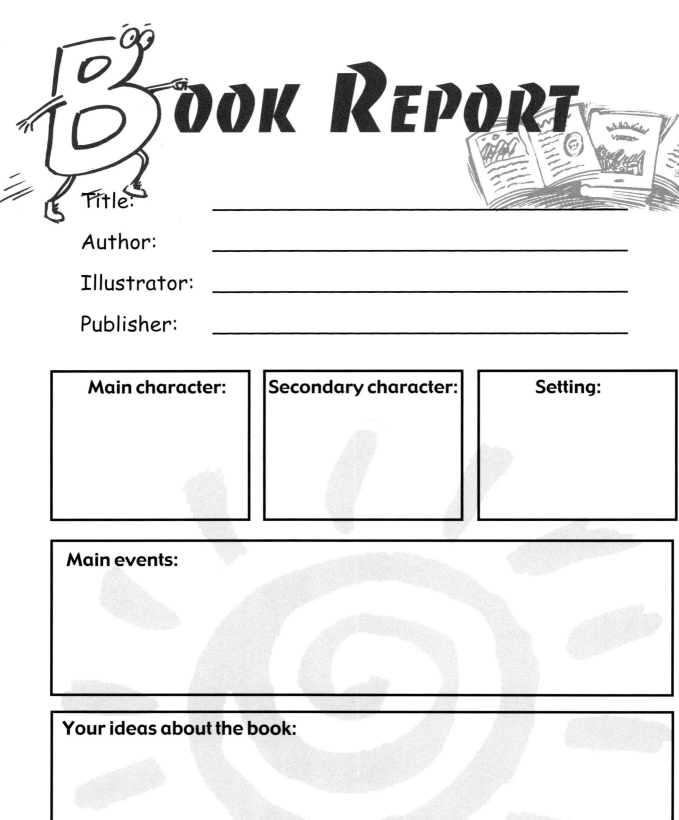

Title: _____

Author: _____

Illustrator: _____

Publisher: _____

Main character:	Secondary character:	Setting:

Main events:

Your ideas about the book:

Name: _____

BOOK REPORT

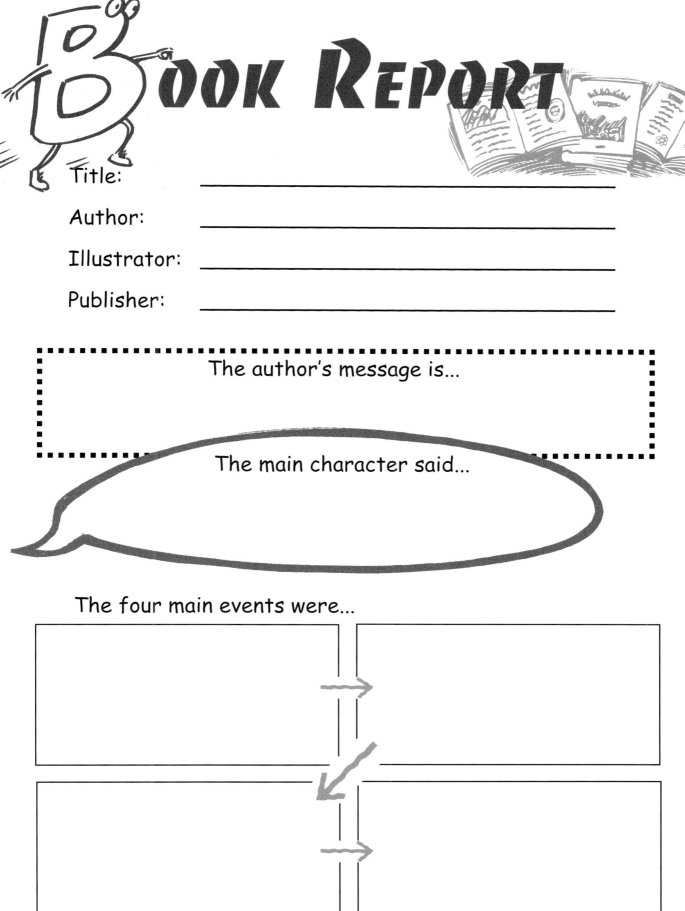

Title: _____

Author: _____

Illustrator: _____

Publisher: _____

The author's message is...

The main character said...

The four main events were...

Name: _____

Book Report

Title: _____

Author: _____

Illustrator: _____

Publisher: _____

Four words to describe this book are:

This book is special because:

Two new words I learned from reading this book are:

_____   _____

My favourite part of the story is...

Name: _____

Thinking about my book...

Title: _____

Author: _____

Illustrator: _____

Publisher: _____

Before you read this book, look at the covers, the title page and the contents page. Think of some questions you would like to ask about the book. Write them down here. Now read the book and write down any answers you find.

Question	Answer

Name: _____